Ann Ward Radcliffe, James Boaden

Fontainville Forest

A Play in Five Acts

Ann Ward Radcliffe, James Boaden

Fontainville Forest
A Play in Five Acts

ISBN/EAN: 9783744692205

Printed in Europe, USA, Canada, Australia, Japan

Cover: Foto ©Thomas Meinert / pixelio.de

More available books at **www.hansebooks.com**

FONTAINVILLE FOREST,

A

PLAY,

IN FIVE ACTS,

(Founded on the Romance of the Foreſt,)

AS PERFORMED AT THE

THEATRE-ROYAL COVENT-GARDEN,

BY

JAMES BOADEN,

OF THE

HONOURABLE SOCIETY OF THE MIDDLE TEMPLE.

It will have blood: they say, blood will have blood.
Stones have been known to move, and trees to speak.
MACBETH.

London.

PRINTED FOR HOOKHAM AND CARPENTER,
NEW BOND STREET.

1794.

TO THAT PUBLIC,

Whose Patronage is an Author's surest Support, as it is his highest Honour, the Play of FONTAINVILLE FOREST *is, with all Respect, dedicated by*

Their most obedient,

Devoted Servant,

JAMES BOADEN.

PROLOGUE.

BY THE AUTHOR OF THE PLAY.

THE Prologue once, indeed, in days of old,
Some previous facts of the new Drama told:
Pointed your expectation to the scene,
And clear'd obstruction, that might intervene:
Possess'd you with those aids, the Author thought
Were requisite, to judge him as you ought.

The moderns, previous hints like these despise,
Demand intrigue, and banquet on surprize:
The Prologue, notwithstanding, keeps its station,
A trembling Poet's solemn lamentation.
Cloak'd up in metaphor, it tells of shocks
Fatal to ships new launch'd, from hidden rocks;
Of critic batteries, of rival strife,
The Destinies that slit the thin-spun life.

Our Author chuses to prepare the way,
With lines at least suggested by his Play.
Caught from the Gothic treasures of Romance,
He frames his work, and lays the scene in France.
The word, I see, alarms—it vibrates here,
And Feeling marks its impulse with a tear.
It brings to thought, a people once refin'd,
Who led supreme the manners of mankind;
Deprav'd by cruelty, by pride inflam'd,
By traitors madden'd, and by sophists sham'd.
Crushing that freedom, which, with gentle sway,
Courted their revolution's infant day,

PROLOGUE.

'Ere giant vanity, with impious hand,
Assail'd the sacred Temples of the Land.

Fall'n is that Land beneath oppression's flood;
Its purest sun has set, alas, in blood!
The milder planet drew from him her light,
And when HE rose no more, soon sunk in night:
The regal source of order, once destroy'd,
Anarchy made the fair creation void.

Britons, to you, by temperate freedom crown'd,
For every manly sentiment renown'd,
The Stage can have no motive to enforce
The principles, that guide your glorious course;
Proceed triumphant—'mid the world's applause,
Firm to your King, your Altars, and your Laws.

DRAMATIS PERSONÆ.

Men.

Marquis of Montault,	Mr. FARREN
Lamotte,	Mr. POPE
Louis,	Mr. MIDDLETON
Peter,	Mr. HULL
Jaques,	Mr. CLAREMONT
Laval,	Mr. BLURTON
Nemours,	Mr. POWELL
Phantom,	Mr. FOLLET.

Women.

Hortensia Lamotte,	Miss MORRIS
Adeline,	Mrs. POPE.

Servants and Guards.

Scene in an Abbey chiefly, and the adjacent parts of the Forest.

Time.—The beginning of the Fifteenth Century.

Note. It was not from a vain tenaciousness that I determined to retain passages expunged in the performance.—The Stage and the Closet are very different mediums for our observance of effects.

FONTAINVILLE FOREST.

ACT I.

SCENE.—*A Gothic Hall of an Abbey, the whole much dilapidated.*

Enter MADAME LAMOTTE, *followed by* PETER.

Madame.

SEEK not to fill me with thefe terrors, Peter:
Here are no figns of any late inhabitants,
The fugitive fears nothing but difcovery.
While we are fafe from all purfuit, no vain
Or fuperftitious fancies fhall difturb me.

   Peter. This is a horrid place, I fcarce dare crawl
Through its low grates and narrow paffages;
And the wind's guft that whiftles in the turrets,
Is as the groan of fome one near his end.
Heaven fend my Mafter back! On my old knees
I begg'd him not explore that difmal wood;
He comforted me then, but fcorn'd my fears.

   Madame. Woud'ft have us perifh here for want?
Have comfort,
Nor let thy Miftrefs teach thee fortitude.

   Peter. Nay, deareft Madam, do not think your old,
But faithful, fervant backward to defend you!

B

From an attack but mortal, against odds
Chearful I'd risk this crazy tenement;
But here my fear is not of human harm.

Madame. May there no greater danger press than your's,
The place will then yield us the needful shelter,
Your master will be safe, and I be happy.
But night is far advanc'd—his absence pains me.

Peter. He went at dusk; by the same token then
The owl shriek'd from the porch—He started back;
But recollected, smote his forehead, and advanc'd;
He struck into the left hand dingle soon:
I clos'd the Abbey gate, which grated sadly.

Madame. Hark! his signal! How! a stranger with him!

[*A knocking against the pannel.*

Enter LAMOTTE *supporting* ADELINE.

Lamotte. Receive this fair unfortunate with kindness.
How she was forc'd to share our wretched fate,
You'll know anon! Peter, go make a fire;
The rain has drench'd our garments through the leaves.
Prepare the supper; our new guest must need
Refreshment.

Madame. Lady, take my arm to assist you.

Adeline. Gratefully.—I was born to trouble others.

Lamotte. Her spirits are violently agitated;
But kindness will restore her mind its tone.
   Madame. Scarce did I ever see a face so beauteous!
   Lamotte. The remark is womanish; I never knew
Distress more poignant—the best reason, wife,
To give our kind assistance and our love.
Bear her in gently—so, now close the doors.
             Exeunt Madame, Adeline, and Peter.

       Manet LAMOTTE.

   Lamotte. Misfortunes thicken on me; sorely pinch'd
By poverty already, I have brought
Another now, to drain away our life-means.
Never admitted to my confidence,
My wife suspects not our decaying store.—
I have reach'd that climax of our wretched being,
When the heart builds no more on heavenly aid.
Despair has laid his callous hand upon me,
And fitted me for deeds, from which I once
Had shrunk with horror—I have no resource
But robbery—The degradation! What!
To nourish guilty life turn common stabber!
Lurk in a hedge, and like an adder sting
The unguarded passenger! Well, and what then?
There's courage in this theft comparatively—
The sharper, routed from the loaded dice,
With which he damns fame, fortune, honour, man,
Rises in morals when he takes the road.

Enter MADAME.

Madame. Lamotte! He seems disturb'd! My
    dearest life!

Lamotte. O, is it you? Reflection on the past
So busied me, I heard not your approach.
How fares the stranger?

Madame. Sunk to startled sleep,
In broken sentences she prays for mercy.
I listen'd while she shriek'd, " Save me! That
    ruffian!
" My father, fly me not!—If I must die,
" Do you dispatch me;—send away that villain."

Lamotte. 'Tis horrible and strange! Her father,
    then,
It was, who forc'd her on me—Listen where.
The evening being calm, I took my walk
To ruminate at full—wrapt up in thought,
Night stole upon me—Through the pathless wild
No signs could I discover that might lead
My erring steps back to this Abbey's towers—
The storm came sudden on, a little while
The shading trees protected me—At length,
A distant taper threw its trembling light
Across the alley where I stood; I ran,
So guided, till I reach'd a paltry cottage.

Madame. 'Twas rash and unadvis'd to venture
    thus.

Lamotte. I knock'd aloud for shelter; from
    within
One ask'd with surly voice my name and business.

I said, a traveller, missing of the road,
And drench'd with rain, begg'd house-room for
 a while.
The man within replied—" Welcome, come in."
I enter'd and advanc'd, when he, in haste,
Clapt to the door and lockt it—Stay, he cried,
I shall return anon! Then from above
Shrieks issued in a female voice—
At length the crazy stairs
Creak'd to the tread of feet, and ent'ring fierce,
A ruffian by the hair dragg'd in a lady;
She seem'd expiring. Stern he bad me swear
To take her from his sight, and ne'er return;
For, if I did, my life should be the forfeit.
I promis'd what he claim'd, and then I told him,
If he would bring us to Fontainville Abbey,
I knew the way from thence—He hid our eyes,
And led us to this gate.
 Madame. Why should a father thus drive out
  his child
To want and wretchedness, or why believe
She will not name him in recover'd reason,
And make the law her refuge? By her dress
She seems to have been taken from some convent,
A holy sister, but not yet profess'd.
 Lamotte. Of this no more; inscrutable to us
The mystery; with her returning sense
We may know all that now perplexes us.
Certain he look'd as little like her father,
As his deeds spoke him—But this well I know,
There is a state of mind, when anguish keen

For vices paft, works on the heart of man,
And wrings it fore, till rifing defperation
Bemonfters quite his nature—then, he fpurns
The ties of blood, cancels all obligation
In which his Maker bound him to his kind,
And is the image of the fiend that tempts him.

   Madame. Heaven ever fhield our hearts from
      fuch defpair!
And yet, Lamotte, I own you wound my foul.
Dark looks, that feek the memory's inward fcrolls,
While the whole outward fenfe is loft, oft mark
Your felf-reproach—If I, by chance, aroufe
And chace you from your mood, your temper
      flames
In caufelefs anger, which you check with fhame,
And wrap you ftraight in filence.

   Lamotte. O, Hortenfia,
I have not liv'd a life can brook diftrefs;
He who is clear within may fmile at ftorms,
And dread no reckoning fhou'd they chance to
      whelm him:
My crimes prefs heavy on me: ftrong compunction,
For miferies entail'd beyond myfelf,
Is feftering here, and when I look on you,
Outcaft for my offences, moody madnefs
   Weighs on my brain, and tells my fhuddering
      foul,
That I am only mark'd out for perdition.
But fee, an angel comes, to whifper peace,
And foothe me with one act of kindnefs render'd!

Enter ADELINE.

Adeline. My honour'd Sir and Madam, I thus press
From short repose, by anguish forc'd upon me,
To pay the thanks your generous pity claims;
For which my heart, in endless gratitude,
Shall daily heave to heav'n, and blessing beg
Upon your heads more bounteous than my own.

Lamotte. Fair Saint, a common benefit like this
Your grateful mind o'erpays.   My lovely daughter,
Chance throws you on a rude and churlish soil,
That cannot yield much medicinal balm,
To heal the wound a parent's hand has dealt you.

Madame. But be of comfort, Lady; as we are,
We live to serve you, while ourselves are safe.
At some fit season of recover'd spirits,
We shall request the story from your lips,
Of what thus orphans you.

Adeline. With willingness,
As far as I have knowledge; but my tale
Is easy told, nor do I know myself,
Why thus I fell under a father's hate.

Lamotte. Of that anon! Now our refreshment calls.
Please you to enter.

Adeline. I have but slender wish
For aught, save rest.—The conflict I have pass'd
Beats at my heart, and fevers every sense.
This friendly solitude, your generous pains,

Will lull the throbbing smart of my affliction,
And give me power to obey you.
   Lamotte. Ever yours.   *[Exeunt.*

       SCENE—*Without the Abbey.*

   Enter from the Gates. (*Morning dawns.*)
  Lamotte. Thus, like the savage lion from his lair,
I wake to prowl for prey. My busy brain
Riots in varied schemes of wickedness,
And drives me from my bed, before the bird,
Whose comfort springs from the return of day.
Light shews me no relief! The morn is fresh;
And hark! the distant hills ring with the sound
Of the glad horn! The hunters are abroad:
I'll dog their chace, and haply seize my prey;
Man, the destroyer, Man, and force the aid,
That misery expects not from his pity.   *[Exit.*

        SCENE—*A Wood.*

    Marquis *and two* Attendants.
  Marquis. The chace fatigues—I'll rest myself awhile—
You to your sport again.—Anon, I'll join you.
                         [Exeunt Attendants.
If we could trust to our presentiments,
I had not ventur'd on the chace to-day.
A tremulous reluctance to the last

Flutter'd about my heart, and now I feel
As if some dreadful certainty of evil
Had led me on to meet impending fate.
Ha! what art thou?
   [*Lamotte rushes in, wild and dishevell'd.*
 Lamotte. A wretch, a very wretch,
Mad with despair, and fell from biting poverty,
Give me the means of life, or take thy death.
 Marquis. Thou'st caught me unawares, I'm in
  thy power.
 Lamotte. Off, off your jewels! Come, your
  purse—dispatch!
Stir not! your life will answer! Followers!
Surprised! Then only speed can save me.
        [*Runs off.*

   Re-enter ATTENDANTS.

 1st Attendant. How's this, my Lord, you look
  aghast with fear?
What wretch was that who fled at our approach?
 Marquis. A robber: Somewhere in these forest
  caves
Most probably he lurks: Command my train,
That there they make strict search to-morrow
  early.
 1st Attendant. Will you know the villain's face
  again, my Lord?
 Marquis. Certain! He look'd not like a common ruffian,
One shrunk from splendour rather—hunted hard

C

By juſtice he had fled, and doom'd to wreſt
His chance ſupport from the lone paſſenger,
Whom, otherways, he harms not—for my life,
Unlike our robbers, he attempted not.

   2d Attendant. He ſhall be found, my Lord, e're
      morrow night,
If here he lurk.—Shall we ſupport you hence?

   Marquis. Alarm has quite enfeebled me—Lead on—
Give up the chace to-day.

   Attendants. This way, my Lord. [*Exeunt.*

SCENE.—*Another part of the Wood.*

Enter LAMOTTE.

   Lamotte. Despair has lent me wings! I've burſt
      my way
Through brake and briar!—Terror has ſteel'd my
      frame!—
I 'ſcap'd unhurt.—Unhurt! O memory,
I'm all one wound, while I yet live to think!
O dearly purchas'd wealth, won by the loſs
Of future peace! Up, damning baubles, up!
Cloſe to the heart, which you have wrung from
      comfort!
Hence, Monſter, hence, nor blot the beauteous
      day!
Hail, cavern'd glooms, to your deep ſhade I fly,
Darkneſs myſelf, to give you living horror. [*Exit.*

END OF THE FIRST ACT.

ACT II.

SCENE—*An Apartment.*

Madame Lamotte. *followed by* Adeline.

Madame.

A Youth appearing much concern'd and eager?
 Adeline. He said he sought in haste a banish'd
  friend,
Whom his conjecture fancied to shroud here.
Fear made me little note his lineaments,
But he seem'd tall and comely.
 Madame. Where's my Lord?
Went he not forth with you this morning early?
 Adeline. Madame, with me! In sooth I have
  not seen him.
 Madame. Indeed! that's strange. I thought he
  might have lur'd
Your contemplation thro' these dreary ruins:
Or giv'n advice, so needful, in the wood,
Apt for concealment.
 Adeline. Dearest lady, hear me!
Forgive me, if I meet your hard suspicion,
And earnest in my vindication, own
I feel at what it points.
 Madame. Nay, pass it by;
For quick interpretation rather shews

A mind that's arm'd by apprehenſion keen,
And trembling for its myſtery, than one
Of conſcious purity, which never guides
Suſpicion's dart unto its deſtin'd aim.

 Adeline. O Madam, I beſeech you, hear your
  ſervant!
If my poor heart harbour a thought of ill,
Or, were it offer'd, would not ſcorn to wrong you,
May heav'n devote me to the ruffian's ſteel,
From which ſo late its providence reliev'd me!—
My ſex's pride *would* arm my breaſt with anger,
And diſdain meet ſuſpicion undeſerv'd;—
But I'm a friendleſs orphan, thrown, alas!
Upon your pity, ſoften'd and ſubdu'd
By miſery unequall'd.—By your peace,
Your ſacred honour! I conjure you, Madam,
Diſmiſs th' unworthy doubts you entertain!
O, be a mother to my tender years,
And form the heart, that's open as the day!

 Madame. My lovely child, I cannot but believe
  you,
And take ſhame on me, that I wrong'd ſuch
  candour.

 Adeline. No more of this—oppreſs me not by
  goodneſs. (*Embracing.*)

 Madame. But I am yet to learn, my Adeline,
How you have paſs'd your youth eſtranged thus
From all parental fondneſs.—If not painful,
Beſeech you ſatisfy me with the tale.

 Adeline. My mother early dying, I was plac'd
Within a neighbour-convent—From my father

Oft I heard, kindly, 'till maturing years
Ask'd for disposal; I was then giv'n to know
His choice assign'd for me the virgin veil,
And banish'd me for ever from the world.

   Madame. The wish was not uncommon; but you found
Objections insurmountable to yielding.

   Adeline. O most weighty were they! I had seen
The sad condition of our sisterhood,
And all their holy spells were lost upon me;
Drawn the so-seeming veil of happiness
From faces, solitude saw wrung with anguish!
A convent is the scene of hopeless tears,
Of heart-struck melancholly, dumb despair,
Of visionary guilt and vain repentance,
Incessant horrors, poor dissimulation.
My heart revolted from it.

   Madame. But your father!
How bore he this refusal?

   Adeline. With displeasure.
At length he fix'd a day to take me thence.
A day, long wish'd for!—but it rose at length
O, day of terrors.—To that house they led me
A destin'd sacrifice—I pray'd, implor'd
In vain!—my senses fled me—on recovery
I was deliver'd to a stranger's care,
Who bore me here, to give my youth a parent.

   Madame. My dearest daughter, you shall find a mother;
And what my fondness can suggest, or yield,
To aid or comfort you, depend on safely.

Enter LAMOTTE.

Lamotte. Is all here safe? On entering just now,
The outer porch, I saw a human figure,
Gliding mysteriously along the hall—
He heard the noise I made; and led thereby,
He follow'd me in haste; I clos'd the trap,
And left him pacing 'cross the gallery
To find the door, by which I 'scap'd his search.

Madame. He, then, it was accosted Adeline,
Without the abbey, in the morning early.

Lamotte. How look'd he?

Adeline. Little like an emissary
Bent to entrap us, but some friendly Guest,
Eager to bring us comfort.

Lamotte. Sure my son!

Louis. (*without.*) Lamotte! Lamotte!

Lamotte. Hush! hark! O senses, mock me not!

Enter LOUIS.

My son! my son! (*embracing him.*)

Louis. My dear, dear father, found
Against all likelihood! My mother too,
My joy o'erpowers me quite! Forgive me, Lady,
 (*To Adeline.*)
The alarm I must have caus'd you, and command
My utmost services.

Adeline. To see you thus

Repaid your pious labour, fills my breaſt
With rapturous feelings never known before.
  Madame. My darling ſon, own an adopted
    ſiſter,
By providence directed to our arms,
To ſoothe and to conſole our lonely life!
Her ſtory you ſhall hear, and weep, at leiſure.
  Louis. I bind her to my heart with deareſt in-
    tereſt.

      Enter PETER *(haſtily.)*

  Lamotte. Now what has chanc'd?
  Peter. Sir, ſince your entrance here,
I hied me to the turret, to obſerve
If any danger menac'd; at ſome diſtance
I ſaw a troop of horſemen ſhape their courſe
Toward the abbey—Be prepar'd, beſeech you!
My dear young maſter too! *(kisses his hand.)*
  Louis. My worthy friend!
Haſte, Peter, to your poſt again; obſerve
All vigilantly.
  Peter. I am gone, dear maſter.   [*Exit.*
  Adeline. Who can they be; Twere beſt you
    hide awhile.
  Lamotte. O there's no need: you find they've
    turn'd aſide;
Travellers, no doubt, who rode up but to gaze
Upon a ruin ſo magnificent.
But tell me, ſon, ſaw you our friend Nemours?
  Louis. He charg'd me, if my ſearch ſhou'd find
    your courſe,

That you'd communicate your views to him,
And let him always know where to addrefs you.
    Lamotte. And I will, Louis, for Nemours, I
        think,
Is fingularly honeft.
    Louis. He's fincere, and plain,
Clear and decifive; knavery alone
Would darken juftice! and the pleader's heart
Should be as open as his face is clofe,
To aid indeed the client he would ferve. (*Violent
        knocking.*)
    Lamotte. Diftraction, I am loft, what's to be
        done?
    Adeline. May I advife, conceal yourfelf below;
We will remain as feeming dwellers here,
And thus difarm fufpicion.
    Louis. Hence, dear father.   [*Exit Lamotte.*

Footfteps heard. Enter the MARQUIS, *who advances. His attendants fill the ftage behind.*

    Marquis. Amazement! Village-rumour, then,
        I fee,
Fell fhort of our new tenants. In me, Lady,
You view the owner of this ruin'd abbey;
Happy, moft happy, if, to you or yours,
It have been ferviceable;—but inftruct me,
How fo much feeming worth cou'd need fuch
        fhelter?
Sirs, you may wait without until I call.
                [*Exeunt Attendants.*

(*Particularly attentive to Adeline.*)

Madame. My Lord, the tale at full were wearisome,
And long it were to tell;—but briefly this,
My husband and myself, our son and daughter,
Compell'd from Paris by misfortune, sought
A shelter from pursuit in this drear spot.

Louis. The inveteracy of our enemies, my Lord,
We hope, ere long, to soften; if meanwhile
Your goodness shall allow this sanctuary,
You bind us ever to your generous pity.

Marquis. Take freely that request—but where's your husband?

A Sliding Pannel opens, LAMOTTE *advances.*

Lamotte. At hand, my Lord, with tears to thank your bounty—(*Seeing the Marquis*)— Ha! swallow me, earth!

[*Starts. Madame runs to support him, the Marquis puts his hand to his sword, and after a few moments turns off as to summon his attendants.*]

Adeline. Beseech you, stay, my Lord!
Lamotte would speak!—my father would explain!

Lamotte. Return! return! My Lord, vouchsafe one word
In private! (*frantically*)

Marquis. You best know whether 'tis prudent
To grant this, after what has past betwixt us.
You can have nought to say, but what with me
Your family may share.

D

Lamotte. By my despair,
I vow these lips shall keep eternal silence,
Ere to another I reveal the tale,
That's due to you alone.

   Marquis. You have your wish.

   Lamotte. First then, my Lord, take this to banish doubt; (*Gives his sword.*)
My life will thus be in your power—But hear me!
I'll lead you to some privacy.

   Marquis. I follow.   [*Exeunt ambo.*

Manent MADAME, ADELINE, LOUIS.

   Madame. What can this mean? Louis, know you the stranger?

   Louis. No; but 'tis probable he may be one
Incens'd against my father from some loss,
Incurr'd by play, and now seeks restitution.

Enter PETER.

   Peter. My Lord's attendants waiting in the hall,
I ask'd them who their master was? They told me
The Marquis of Montault—he has a castle
Hard by here, and these, our apartments now,
Were long since furnish'd as a hunting lodge,
To accommodate the present Lord's late brother.

   Adeline. Madam, let me beseech you to retire,
Their difference I doubt not is compos'd.

   Madame. I'm lost in wonder at it—O my husband!   [*Exeunt.*

SCENE—*A remote Apartment.*

Enter LAMOTTE—MARQUIS.

Marquis. This place has privacy to suit your purpose.
Speak, I am all attention.
Lamotte. O my Lord,
Pity the agonies you see me suffer!
Have mercy on a wretch, whose poverty
Stung him to madness! At your feet I fall
Submissive to your sentence—Spare my life!
And think my crime atton'd by these deep horrors!
O save a family that never wrong'd you!
All, all shall be restor'd—If worlds could buy
That peace of mind with which I enter'd here,
I'd silence my compunction by the gift.
Marquis. Rise, Sir, take back your sword, and hear my answer.
You may be worth my clemency, and I
Incline to spare you—but at least some test
Should prove your deep repentance of the crime.
Lamotte. If my whole life, with zeal devoted to you,
Can but atone, expose it to all hazards,
None will I shrink from you may point me to,—
So you but add your silence to forgiveness.
Marquis. Extravagant professions I regard not.
The first test I exact from you is truth.

D 2

Who is that lovely maid I saw but now?
Is she your daughter?

Lamotte. No, my Lord, she is not.
Chance threw her on my care; an orphan friend-
 less,
And, but for me, devoted by a ruffian,
To savage slaughter.

Marquis. Well, Lamotte, this fair one
May heal the breach between us—She has beauty
That struck me at first sight—I'll see her shortly.
Excuse my prompt departure to your wife,
And lead her to expect my frequent visits.
Our discord may be stil'd mistake, explain'd
At length, and settled into friendship.—For
'Tis with yourself, to fix, or loose the bands.
Lamotte, good night.

Lamotte. I rest your grateful servant, [*Exeunt.*

SCENE.—*Another Apartment,*

MADAME LAMOTTE.

Madame. How painful this suspense! How
 strange the cause!
I've lost myself in crude and wild conjecture,
And find no clue to dreadful certainty.
One thing indeed seems likely—this late shock,
And his past melancholy, spring alike
From one, one fatal source. My husband comes!
O how this interval has wrung my soul!

Enter LAMOTTE.

Where is the Marquis?

Lamotte. Gone—Now to prepare
For interrogatories, springing all
From raging curiosity, that fever,
Which dries up all the virtue of your sex!

Madame. I pardon a reproach I feel unmerited.
Nor would I urge you to unwilling converse.
For I would soothe your mind, not irritate
Its secret wounds—but answer me this question,
Did your late terror spring from the same cause
As all before it?

Lamotte. Woman, forbear your questions!
I have no temper, or to hear, or answer.
Have I not long forbidden you to mention,
Or hint even at this subject?

Madame. Hint at what?

Lamotte. O, true. I thought you had mentioned it before.

Madame. Nay then, I must suspect my notion grounded.

Lamotte. Suspect not, nor enquire; for 'twill be fruitless.
Whate'er the cause of my late wild emotions,
I will not now disclose it. Time may come
Concealment will no more be necessary.

Madame. A needless caution tow'ards your fond
 Hortensia;
But do your pleasure.

Lamotte. In the mean time, this—

Note not to any aught uncommon in me;
Bury suspicion deep in your own breast,
As you'd avoid our ruin and my curses.

[*Exeunt.*

SCENE.—*An Apartment.*

ADELINE *alone.*

Adeline. I've heard of fix'd antipathies in minds,
And mortal loathing to peculiar objects!
No cause to be assign'd but shudd'ring nature!
I feel it is so: for my very soul
Sicken'd at yonder Marquis—Yet he look'd
Dispos'd to do me kindness, much observant;
Hated civility, observance painful!
'Tis like we see him often, while his pity
Continues to Lamotte this place of shelter.
Well, what of that? Improvident alarm!
I can retire then to my chamber—How! [*Knock.*
One knocks.

Enter LOUIS.

Louis. My Adeline, may I intrude
To tell you what hath chanc'd since you retir'd?
Adeline. Most welcome.
Louis. Then, the Marquis is set off,
In seeming kindness, and my father now
Withdrawn to his Apartment much disturb'd.
Adeline. Where is my gracious lady, your dear
　　mother?
Louis. Also retir'd—At his return, in sorrow,

She question'd on the cause of his late horror,
And I o'erheard him loudly chide her love.

Adeline. Alas, dear lady, how my heart bleeds
    for her!
I never knew the comfort of a mother
Until her kindness rous'd the filial fondness.

Louis. O think, sweet, tender saint, my feel-
    ings for her!
When home return'd from the alarms of war,
Mine from my earliest youth, I found that home
Seiz'd on by legal harpies, while its lord,
A fugitive, had stol'n away by night
From the dread ills of passion unrestrain'd.
Think of these stigmas on a soldier's pride,
Flush'd with the darling fame of victory!

Adeline. Yes, I can feel the disappointing an-
    guish.
But let not this reproof decrease our love:
My brother, I'm so much indebted there,
That life can yield no means of recompence
To the preserver of this injur'd being.

Louis. Would only I had been so blest, to prove
The saviour of distressed Adeline!

Adeline. And let me say, were I again to need
    one,
I know not any friend to whom my heart
Would with more pleasure pay its gratitude.

Louis. Transporting sounds! O let me not be
    thought
Presuming, if I thus discard the mask,

Which ill conceals the love that is my glory!
My soul is yours.

'*Adeline.* For your esteem I thank you,
' Deeply, believe me;—but your own good sense
' Will teach you how improper the pursuit
' Of one like me, with passion so ill-judg'd.—
' You see I throw away all coy reserve,
'. And do not ev'n affect to miss your meaning.

'*Louis.* My heart is bounden to your generous
' candour;
' Yet how can I forbear to speak of that,
' Which flows thro' and informs my very being?'

Adeline. Your pardon—here I end this conference—
I beg I may be spar'd—I would not hear
Aught that may shake my best opinion of you.

Louis. Farewell, my Adeline; may spirits of peace
Settle upon that bosom in repose,
And fancy, if she stirs beneath their wings,
Present my love obedient to your will.   [*Exit.*

Adeline. (after a pause.) The night is rough,
    and through these shatter'd casements,
The wind in shrilling blasts sweeps the old hangings.
Whether the place alone puts such thoughts in me,
I know not; but asleep, or waking, still
Conviction haunts me, that some mystery
Is wrapt within these chambers, which my fate
Will have me penetrate.—The falling gust

With feeble tone expires like dying sighs—
The tap'stry yonder shakes, as tho' some door
Open'd behind it (*takes her lamp*) Ha! 'tis so;
    the bolt,
Tho' rusty, yields unto my hand; I'll see
To what it leads.—How, if I sink with fear?
And so benumb'd, life freeze away in horror?
No matter, powerful impulse drives me onward,
And my soul rises to the coming terror.   [*Exit.*

SCENE—*changes to a melancholy Apartment. The Windows beyond reach, and grated.—An old Canopy in the distance, with a torn Set of Hanging-Tapestry.*

Enter ADELINE.

Adeline. I must be cautious, lest the sudden blast
Extinguish my faint guide. ' I'll place the lamp
' Behind this sheltering bulk.'—What's this I
    tread on?
A dagger, all corroded by the rust!
Prophetic soul! Yes, murder has been busy!
A chilly faintness creeps across my heart,
And checks the blood that strives in vain to follow.
               [*Pause, sits down.*
I feel recover'd, and new strength is giv'n me!
'Tis destiny compels,—On to my task.
Yon tatter'd ruin yawns to tempt enquiry.
            [*Touches it, all falls down.*
What scroll thus meets me in the falling lumber?

Let me examine it: blurr'd all by damps;
Mouldy, in parts illegible. I'll hence now:
The waning light warns me to gain my chamber.
Inspire me, great Avenger! Angels guard me!
[*Exit.*

THE END OF THE SECOND ACT.

ACT III.

SCENE.—*An Apartment.*

Enter ADELINE.

Adeline.

I MUST conceal yon parchment till I fee
What it contains.—Madame Lamotte approaches.
The terrors that have hover'd o'er my flumbers,
May well alone account for my disturbance.

Enter MADAME LAMOTTE.

Madame. Good morrow, deareft daughter—but how's this?
You look, my love, in a diforder'd ftate,
As though alarm had ruffled your repose.
‘ *Adeline.* 'Tis likely, Madam,—for the night
‘ has pafs'd
‘ In vifions fo bewildering, and dreadful,
‘ That Nature fhudders under their impreffion.'
O my lov'd mother, I have firm conviction,
That fome attrocious act has ftain'd this place,
In which my fate will have me interefted.
Madame. But tell, what thus leads you to infer fo?
‘ What were thofe vifions?'
Adeline. I had fcarcely funk
In flumber, when my fancy's bufy range
Produc'd before me thefe connected horrors.

Methought, within a 'wretched old apartment,
A dying Cavalier, weltering in blood,
Lay stretch'd upon the floor.—By name he call'd
   me,
A deadly paleness spread o'er all his features;
Yet look'd he most benign, with mingled love,
And majesty. While thus I gaz'd upon him,
His face seem'd struck with death; the chilly dews
And shuddering agonies came on.—I started—
He seized me with convulsive violence—
Striving to disengage my hand, once more
I caught his eye, it brighten'd into glory!
He gaz'd on me with fondness—his lips mov'd,
As they would speak—but then the opening
   ground
Gave him swift way, and shut him from my sight.
   ' *Madame.* My dear, dear child, the Abbey's
    ' constant gloom,
' Or the rude terrors of the day gone by,
' Doubtless impress'd these fancies on your mind.
  ' *Adeline.* O but they ceas'd not there.—Mark
   ' the coherence.
' Again I dreamt—I thought before me pass'd
' One cloth'd in black, as for some funeral rite.
' He beckon'd me—I follow'd till he came
' Unto a bier, upon the which lay dead
' The person seen before.—As I approach'd,
' A stream of blood well'd from his wounded side,
' And fill'd the chamber—groans then smote my
   ' ear;

' Again one call'd upon me :—Horror's hand
' Grasp'd me so strongly, that I sudden wak'd,
' Nor could convince myself that I had dream'd,
' The agonizing vision did so shake me.'
 Madame. I would not have you yield to such
  illusions;
They do usurp the pow'rs, that make life happy,
And thickly cloud the sunshine of the mind.
Think no more of them. But, my Adeline,
Know you what late hath pass'd? My Lord, the
  Marquis,
Is now so fast our friend, that he bestows
Not merely this concealment, but his interest
On our behalf, and means to see us often.
 Adeline. Believe me, I rejoice at aught may add
To your content, ev'n should it marr my own.
 Madame. Lamotte reports, my Adeline, such
  praise
Express'd of your appearance by the Marquis,
As led him to believe the warmth of love
Inspir'd the proud eulogium.
 Adeline. Compliment,
Mere compliment, I doubt not; for the Marquis
Is of the stamp of fashion, current oft
With fair profession of dissembled worth.
 Madame. Nay, I should chide these prepossess-
  sions, love;
The Marquis now is our approved friend.
 Adeline. I know it—But if I might be indulg'd
In absence when he visits here, my heart,
And yet I know not why, would feel the lighter.

Enter LOUIS.

Louis. Madam, the Marquis juſt arriv'd below,
In converſe with my father, begs the honour
To pay in perſon his reſpects.—He hopes
The lovely Adeline will there attend you.

Madame. We come immediately.—My dear, go
 down—
I'll join you inſtantly—Louis, a word.
 [*Exit with Louis.*

Adeline. I go : Be ſtill, ye buſy apprehenſions !
Now to conceal lurking antipathy
Beneath the guize of lowly gratitude ;
O when will clear integrity be mine,
That ſafely may diſdain to *look* a falſehood ?
 [*Exit.*

SCENE—*Another Apartment.*

Enter MARQUIS *and* LAMOTTE.

Marquis. In ſhort, Lamotte, perſuade her to
 compliance ;
You may acquaint her too, that her fierce father,
Repenting that he ſpar'd her, claims his child,
And that my power alone protects her from him.
Be firm my advocate, and I conſent
To wave reſentment for my injuries.

Lamotte. In this and all things I obey with
 zeal.—
She's coming down—I'll leave you ſoon together;
Coyneſs is ſtronger made by company.

Enter ADELINE.

Now mark me, Adeline—You know our fum
Of obligation to this generous Lord;
He honours you with fentiments of love;
Hear them attentively, and fo determine,
As beft becomes your prudence, our condition.
[*Exit.*

Marquis. My charming Adeline, at length my
 fortune
Indulges me with opportunity,
To pour the tendereft paffion out before you,
And thus declare the conqueft you have made.

Adeline. So little known, my Lord, I take no
 pride
In the diftinction, for it tells me plainly
'Twas but a worthlefs outfide has procur'd it.

Marquis. Nay, wrong me not, for from the
 exterior fhew
Of all perfection, fhould we not infer
The purity within, that gives the whole
Its harmony and grace?

Adeline. O, what a world
Were this, how excellently fair and perfect,
Did through its beauteous mafs, no canker creep,
To infect, unfeen, the lovelinefs of nature!

Marquis. Why feek to dim the luftre of thofe
 eyes,
Why throw a flur upon Creation's pride,
The matchlefs treafure of her bounty, now
Lock'd in the winning form of Adeline?

Adeline. In flattery, the so be-praised maid
Ne'er found one charm to lift her self-esteem:
Hear me ingenuously, while I lay
The simple dictates of my heart before you.
 ' *Marquis.* Nay, now at least, I may in turn
  ' object
' Precipitation, since you know not yet
' The grounds on which your wisdom should de-
 ' cide.'
Adeline. For your attention I am grateful, Sir,
But I should wrong the truth, myself and candour,
If, confident that I can never change,
I did not now decline the good you mean me.
 Marquis. This is the language of your inexpe-
  rience.
Consider well your situation here,
Expos'd to share the perils that surround
A banish'd man—With me you will partake
The elegance of life, and all the joys
That base and sordid penury repines at.
' No wish that e'er can rise within the heart
' Of still desiring woman, but my care
' Shall strive to anticipate, 'ere words be giv'n it.'
 Adeline. My Lord, you tempt me not by phrase
  like this.
Such as myself, seasoned within the school
Of poverty, nor covet, nor regard
A splendour, commonly the foe to virtue,
' What most I wish for, is to be allow'd
' Th' indulgence of this solitude awhile,
' To heal the wounds so deep inflicted here.'

Marquis. This lonely place will rather fix a gloom
For ever on your youth, that should be led
To happier scenes of gay, voluptuous love.
   Adeline. I thank you, Sir, for thus at once displaying
The glaring infamy design'd for me!
An honourable purpose had received
At least my gratitude ev'n in rejection;
But this, for its mean insult, has my scorn.
                                              [*Exit.*
   Marquis. Stay, I conjure you! Hear me Adeline!
She's gone, and plainly understood my purpose.
Well, well, my saucy virtue, we shall find
Decoys may lure this soaring bird to stoop;
And snatch at offer'd marriage—Now, Lamotte!

              Enter LAMOTTE.

   Lamotte. How's this, my Lord; went she in anger from you?
   Marquis. Even but now—She's better fortified
Than I expected: young and beautiful,
I look'd that raptures would have caught her taste;
But she's of cold and prudish temperature,
And feigns to hate the ardour she solicits.
   Lamotte. I fear you spoke too plainly; Adeline
Is convent-bred, to be approach'd by slow,
And seeming pure devotion—nor, until
The holy ritual sanctifies embrace,
Will she e'er sink the saint in willing woman.

F

Marquis. 'Tis plain; she hinted marriage: be it so.
When next I meet her, we must wear a face
Of soberer meaning. Do you lead her think
What pass'd was but the froth of gallantry—
Harmless, tho' warm, the language of the world.

Lamotte. Only, my Lord, be cautious of Hortensia!
Once in her breast the flame of jealousy
Was kindled on this girl's account; but now
She loves her so entirely, that her rashness
Would frustrate all.

Marquis. That should indeed be heeded:
For, in despite of all this swelling anger,
She must be mine by kindness, or by force.

[*Exeunt.*

SCENE—*An Apartment.*

Enter LOUIS *and* PETER.

Louis. How say'st thou, Peter—one brought here by night,
And close confin'd?

Peter. The neighbours say so closely,
That no one ever saw him afterward;
This did I learn here hard by, at Auboine:
And they do add, that here he sure was murder'd,
And no one since has slept within the abbey.

Louis. Did any guess who the deceased was?

Peter. No—none cou'd e'er conjecture aught about him.

Louis. When did this happen?

Peter. Why, about the time
The prefent Marquis came to his eftates,
On the demife of the late Lord, his brother.

Louis. Where then did he die?

Peter. O, abroad they fay;
Slain in the field—but for the man confin'd,
By flow degrees the rumour died away,
And all enquiry ceas'd.

Louis. A ftrange adventure!

Peter. My dear young mafter, if I not miftake,
Nought that refpects the lovely Adeline
To you will be indifferent—Of late
I have o'erheard my mafter and yon Marquis
In deep cabal, and fhe the fubject of it:
Much do my fears inform me, out of hints
And broken fentences, that harm is meant her.

Louis. My worthy friend, I thank thee. Yes, indeed,
Deep is the intereft I feel for her;
But fure my father never would confent
To aught of violent means—I know the Marquis,
Follows with eyes of love, her fweet perfections,
And hopes his rank and fplendour may allure her.

Peter. But fhe endures him not—This very morn
She left him difcompos'd, her lovely cheek
Flufh'd with the anger of infulted virtue.

Louis. You muft be vigilant—You know the pow'r
And danger too that wait about this Lord.

Peter. O fear me not. The fenfe of apprehenfion
Is quicken'd by the body's feeblenefs—

F 2

But I am old and worthless, and, sweet master,
Were my last throb of life to flit away
In the dear cause of innocence oppres'd,
How could my death have better preparation?

Louis. No more of this just now. I'll to the
 Marquis,
For I must seem attentive while he stays;
And sure this stormy night will here detain him.

Peter. I'll bring you what intelligence I glean
From his domestics to your honour's chamber.
[*Exit.*

Louis. Farewell, then, and be trusty, my good
 fellow.

Enter LAMOTTE.

Lamotte. Now, Sir, what tale of folly have you
 glean'd
From yonder babbler?

Louis. Nothing I regard much.
He was recounting the credulity
Of the near hamlet, touching this our dwelling.

Lamotte. All fabulous, I doubt not. Some one
 murder'd,
And that stale lie, a spirit following it.

Louis. Somewhat indeed of that kind was the story;
You know it to be idle by experience,
Longer at least than mine.

Lamotte. O idle all!

Louis. And yet they could not well have been
 mistaken
In one so brought here!

Lamotte. No, not well, I think.

Louis. 'Tis likeliest they removed him hence by night.

Lamotte. Most likely.

Louis. For we should not rashly credit
A rumour might throw scandal on a friend.

Lamotte. No, by no means. That mouldering chest I saw—

Louis. How!

Lamotte. Did I say I saw it? I mistook, boy;
'Tis said, contains a body, which still lies
Unburied in the secret chamber.

Louis. Still!
Have you then seen the relics of the man,
Said to have perished here?

Lamotte. Who, I, my son?
Not I—I say again, 'tis the report.

Louis. My father is unwell.

Lamotte. Much indispos'd!
Somewhat now raps me, and my busy brain
Is cross'd with incoherency unusual.
Say, have you lately look'd abroad, my son?

Louis. But now. The gathering gloom is deep'ning round,
And every sign foretells a dreadful shock
Of elemental war—Our noble guest
Stays in the abbey, I presume, to-night?

Lamotte. He does. O, Louis—'twere good that you endeavour'd
To chace that fev'rish tale from Peter's brain;
If he should e'er possess the women with it,

Our time would pass delightfully indeed.
 Louis. To-morrow, with your leave, I shall
  set out
For Paris on affairs concern us nearly.
 Lamotte. I had forgot. Nemours I'll write to,
  then—
You shall bear my letter. No, the Marquis
Must not, in thought, be tainted by these ru-
  mours! (*Aside.*)
Attend me to my chamber—Mystery all! (*Aside.*)
        [*Exeunt.*

SCENE—*The secret Apartment, gloomy and rude, only clear'd of the Lumber formerly there.*

    Adeline alone.
 Adeline. At last I am alone! And now may
  venture
To look at the contents of this old manuscript.
A general horror creeps thro' all my limbs,
And almost stifles curiosity. (*Reads.*)
 " The wretched Philip, Marquis of Montault,
 " Bequeaths his sorrows to avenging time.
 " O you, whate'er ye are of human kind,
 " To whom this sad relation of my woes
 " Shall come, afford your pity to a being,
 " Shut from the light of day, and doom'd to
  perish."——
O Heav'n, the dagger! Yes, my fears were
  founded.
 " They seiz'd me as I reach'd the neighbour
  wood,

" Bound and then brought me here; at once I
 knew
" The place, the accurs'd design, and their em-
 ployer,
" Yet, O my brother, I had never wrong'd you."
His brother! What, yon Marquis?
 Phantom. Even he. *(heard within the chamber.)*
 Adeline. Hark! Sure I heard a voice! No, 'tis
  the thunder
That rolls its murmurs thro' this yawning pile.
 " They told me I should not survive three days,
 " And bade me choose, or poison, or the sword;
 " O God, the horrors of each bitter moment!
 " The ling'ring hours of day, the sleepless
  night!
 " Eternal terrors in a span of life!
Poor, wretched sufferer! Accept the tears
Of one, like thee, pursued by fortune's frown,
Yet less unhappy!
 Phantom. O, Adeline! *(faintly visible.)*
 Adeline. Ha! sure I'm call'd! No, all are now
  at rest.
How powerful is fancy! I'll proceed.
 " At length I can renew this narrative.
 " To leave no means untempted of escape,
 " I climb'd these grated windows, but I fell
 " Stunn'd and much bruis'd, insensate to the
  ground.
 " The day allotted dawns! Ye boding terrors,
 " I feel to-morrow I shall be as nothing!

Great God of mercy! could there none be found
To aid thee? Then he perish'd—

Phantom. Perish'd here.

Adeline. My sense does not deceive me! awful
sounds!
'Twas here he fell!

[*The phantom here glides across the dark part of
the Chamber, Adeline shrieks, and falls back.
The Scene closes upon her.*

THE END OF THE THIRD ACT.

ACT IV.

SCENE—*The Hall* (*dark.*)

Violent Thunder and Light'ning, the Abbey rocks, and through the distant Windows one of the Turrets is seen to fall, struck by the Light'ning.

Enter the MARQUIS, *wild and dishevell'd.*

Marquis.

AWAY! Pursue me not! Thou Phantom, hence!
For while thy form thus haunts me, all my powers
Are wither'd as the parchment by the flame,
And my joints frail as nervelefs infancy.
(*Light'ning.*)
See, he unclafps his mangled breast, and points
The deadly dagger.—O, in pity strike
Deep in my heart, and fearch thy expiation;
Have mercy, mercy! *(falls upon his knee.)* Gone!
    'tis all illusion!
O no! If images like these are fanciful,
The griding rack gives not such real pain.
My eyes have almost crack'd their strings in wonder,
And my swoln heart so heaves within my breast,
As it would bare its secret to the day.
'Twas sleep that unawares surpriz'd me yonder,
And mem'ry lent imagination arms,

G

To probe my ulcerous spirit to the quick.
I'll tarry here no longer. Ho! Lamotte!
Awake! awake! The horrors of the night
Alone would banish slumber from the pillow
Of quiet innocence.

Enter LAMOTTE.

Lamotte, forgive me,
For thus disturbing you! I've just rememb'red
A pressing business, that now claims me hence,
And will not bear the least delay.—I'll on.

Lamotte. The storm is yet tremendous! wait awhile,
Until the fury of its rage be past.

Marquis. Not a moment! Without! Prepare my horses!
Lamotte, to-morrow I'll return by noon.
Now then, good night to both.

Lamotte. Good night, my Lord. [*Exit Marquis.*
How deadly pale he looks!   (*Aside.*)
Ay, ay. 'tis so. (*Aside.*)   [*Exit.*

SCENE.

Enter ADELINE *and* LOUIS.

Adeline. Thus have I made you the depositary
Of all I think or know of yonder villain.
Now then determine, as your love of justice,
With any softer argument to aid it,
May lead you.

Louis. Lovely Adeline, my father

I fear so strictly in this monster's gripe,
That we must act without his privity.
Do you entrust this parchment to my care;
I am bound for Paris, there to await Nemours,
My father's advocate: unto his honesty
We may confide this evidence of guilt.

   Adeline. I think with you—But, O my friend,
      I doubt not
Attempts will yet be made to shake my purpose,
Perhaps to wound my honour.

   Louis. Shall I stay,
And bulwark with my life, its dearest blessing?
No danger can be terrible for thee.
Speak but the word, and I refuse the journey.

   Adeline. Nay, let no thought of me withhold
      your purpose;
My boding spirit tells me that a great,
A mighty vengeance works to punish guilt?
Shall my weak fears prevent or thwart its aim?
No! For against all artifice I am steel'd
By horror and aversion; and the force
That violates my honour, quenches life;
They never can be sunder'd.

   Louis. O my Adeline,
Thus bowing to your will, 'ere I depart,
Let me breathe out the fervour of one pray'r,
For your prosperity and lasting peace.
And might my death even prove the happy means
To give your merits their due share of ho‑‑‑‑,
The martyr's crown were not more wel‑‑‑‑‑
     him.

Adeline. Adieu, my brother, prosperous be your journey!

Louis. May angels, not more fair, (for, can they be so?)
But, pure as thou art, bless thee, and preserve thee.
[*Exeunt severally.*

SCENE—*The Hall.*

Enter LAMOTTE *and* MADAME.

Lamotte. Louis may here be spar'd.—Hortensia, tell me,
Has it ne'er struck you, that my son had felt
The charms of Adeline? become their captive?
I have observ'd he gazes oft' upon her—
Has frequent absences; while melancholly
Presses his spirit to her sullen breast,
And chains the gay, and quick alacrity
Of his once happy nature.

Madame. It may be so,
For she has beauty might allure the feet
Of laggard age, to pace the round of courtship,
And virtues that would give the firmest base,
For wedded bliss to spring from—And were I
To choose a daughter from contending maids,
My choice——

Lamotte. Should never fall on Adeline;
I sent the boy hence to avoid the ruin,
A passion so perverse wou'd bring on us.
The Marquis doats upon her: think the rest,
Were he to find a rival in my son!

Madame. Something of this before you touch'd
 on to me;
But I am yet to know Montault's design:
For to espouse her, that, my fears inform me,
His dignity disdains—and ought below this
Would be, deservedly, by her rejected.
 Lamotte. He may be brought to wed her. But,
  Hortensia,
Has she in confidence e'er given you up
The nature of his first proposals to her?
 Madame. Never. Indeed her hatred seems so
  rooted,
That I avoid the subject, which most wrings
Her placid temper from its calm of sweetness.
 Lamotte. The sex, the precious sex! still apt
  to fly
The object, wisdom woos them to accept,
And court, in madness, beggary and love!
Spurning all guests but such as make them
 wretched;
Infatuate folly ruling their affections,
Is the epitome of womankind.
 Madame. Then you would aid the Marquis's
  designs?
 Lamotte. Would! Nay, I must.
 Madame. Lamotte, consider first
Whether that best friend, Conscience, will allow it.
 Lamotte. I have no time for craven thoughts
  like these.
A lot like mine needs powerful supporters;

Chance throws them in my way, and would'st
    thou have
A school-boy's terror make me shrink to clasp
    them?
 Madame. Chance threw, too, in your way a
    helpless orphan,
You did not snatch her from the ruffian's dagger,
Nor bear her from a most disnatur'd father,
To yield her beauty to the lust of greatness;
And save her life but to destroy her honour.
 Lamotte. O, what I find you are of their mystery,
The confidante of this illustrious passion!
Which, to indulge the mother's hopeful boy!
Devotes the needless Sire to certain ruin.
 Madame. Not so, my husband. We have here
    obtain'd
A shelter from the perils which you fled;
But greater may be found even in safety,
If feeling fall a sacrifice to interest.
 Lamotte. No more of this I charge you.—Must
    I stand,
And hear with temper lectures thus compos'd
By kindred frailty and injurious fondness?
 Madame. Neither of these have led me to suggest
What you thus taunt.—I am myself a mother,
I feel the crowding hopes, the anxious fears,
The sorrows, and the transports of a mother!
I were unworthy of that sacred name,
Could I stand by, and see one mother's joy
Basely betray'd to misery and guilt.   [*Exit.*

Lamotte. Confusion! So, Hortensia then suspects
The Marquis may play false—and hints dishonour
On such as tamely give his passion scope.
My crimes have wound his toils so fast around me,
I dare not thwart his purpose.—Tempt her for
  him!
Poison her mind! that when the real snake
Encircles her fair form, he may be welcom'd!
No, by my guilt I will not be that fiend.
What, if I trust to further explanation?
He may desist from fondness misapplied,
And quit with high disdain her cold rejection.—

   Enter PETER.

Peter. One of the Marquis's attendants now
Is just arriv'd—He brings intelligence
His Lord will on the instant reach the Abbey.
        [*Exit.*

Lamotte. I will attend him. Yes, it shall be so;
Tho' deeply sunk by wrongs of less account,
Conscience, not quite extinguish'd, starts with
  horror
At such a crime as this! O may it work,
Till sweet contentment heal my tortur'd breast.
        [*Exit.*

  SCENE—*Adeline's Apartment.*

   ADELINE *alone.*

Adeline. From the Oriel window, I discern'd
  just now

The Marquis's arrival, and Lamotte
Haftening to give him welcome—Some ftrong
    chain
So links him to yon villain's intereft,
I dare not flatter me, his pity e'er
Would crofs his patron's will, to fuccour me.
'Tis likely I fhall foon be fummon'd down
To meet new infults—Some one now approaches—
'Tis my tormentor—'tis Montault himfelf.

Enter MARQUIS.

Marquis. You will, no doubt, feel fomewhat
    of furprize,
That, after the contempt which lately met me,
I court again unwilling conference.
But the rude treatment which my paffion found,
Convinces me its tenour was miftaken,
And I forget indignity unmerited.
   Adeline. I'm glad, ev'n now, to hear its fting
    difclaim'd!
Language as grofs as fenfual man e'er utter'd,
Found from me but the fcorn it well deferv'd.
   Marquis. Believe me, lovelieft Adeline, no
    thought,
But fuch as modeft Hymen well might fanction,
E'er fprung within the bofom that adores you.
Explicit declaration beft may ferve
To aid my love, and fhape your refolution.
I offer you my fortune with my hand.
   Adeline. Were the gay knot to bind me to the
    wealth

Of all the world, ev'n at the offer'd inftant,
I fhould at once inflexibly reject it.

 ' *Marquis.* 'Tis then as I fufpected; prepof-
  ' feffion
' So rooted and unyielding, takes its date
' From fome more favour'd paffion—Ay, why
  not
' Yon Boy, my eafy nature has permitted
' To fting my breaft uncrufh'd.

 ' *Adeline.* Nay, hear me, Marquis,
' May there not be fome other caufe more ftrong
' Than preference, to ftimulate rejection?

 ' *Marquis.* None. When the courted fhrine of
  vanity
' Is heap'd with offerings of unbounded wealth,
' If prudence did not dictate their acceptance,
' Virtue would thus fecure the fplendid means
' Of fuccouring the miferies arround her.'

 Adeline. What! to become more miferable far
Than any caufe external e'er cou'd make her?
Know, that a tranquil bofom is the good
Which virtue deareft prizes, and when wealth
Courts her reluctant gratitude in vain,
She fpurns it, and remains in peace, tho' poor.

 Marquis. You but deceive yourfelf.—' Survey
  the world,
' Its daily tribes of wedded facrifices!
' Moft to fuppofed neceffity give up
' The boon withheld from humble, faithful love.
' The Great are intereft's perpetual flaves,
' And live, and act, and think alone for others.

H

' *Adeline.* This is no novel doctrine, nor I need
  ' not
' Such arguments as thefe to mould my purpofe.
' I never can be yours.
  ' *Marquis.* You muſt—You will.
' By all my love, I charge you tempt me not
' By fuch rejection, to abufe my power.
' I would perfuade by honourable means,
' But once defied, may fall on lower forms.'
    Adeline. My Lord, I beg you leave me! nor
      provoke
The language muſt difpleafe you.
    Marquis. No! Ev'n now
My paſſion chides me for this dull delay,
And bids me feize the tempting treafure here,
Nor idly wafte entreaties when my pow'r
May force compliance.
    Adeline. Hear me, I conjure you.
    Marquis. I have heard too much; and my im-
      petuous love
Now grafps its choiceſt good——In vain this
    ſtruggle!
How lovely is this terror! By my tranfport
It heightens the bewitching charm of beauty,
And lends ten thoufand graces to that bofom.
    Adeline. Help! help! for mercy's fake.
    Marquis. You call in vain.
None dare intrude. Know, here, that I command;
No power on earth fhall fnatch you from my arms—
        (*He purfues her, and feeing the picture of her
          mother, fnatches it from her bofom.*)

Ha! what is this? Hell! do my eyes deceive me?
My brother's wife! Even as she liv'd once more!
 Adeline. Then my father's murderer stands before me.
 Marquis. Thou shadowy Minister of punishment!
Why does thy withering power of curs'd resemblance
Now start before my sight to blast my joys?
Art thou sent here by him, whose phantom form
In horrid vengeance hurried me to madness?
Or is there yet some living instrument
To punish fratricide? Thou, who haft thus
Unmann'd my soul, tell me, I charge thee, truly,
Whose the resemblance that is now before me?
 Adeline. My mother's!
 Marquis. Dreadful certainty!
How to resolve, as yet I know not; but
My better angel bids me to beware,
And make all sure. Yes, this shall be her prison.
Distracting thoughts so crowd upon my brain,
That all is chaos, frenzy and despair. [*Exit.*
 Adeline. Amazement wraps my senses! Gracious God,
In awful sorrow I adore thy justice!
Protector of the Orphan, O direct me!
And lead the Child, miraculously sav'd,
To pull down vengeance on her father's murd'rer.
          [*Exit.*

SCENE—*The Wood.*

Enter the MARQUIS *and* LAMOTTE.

Marquis. Lamotte, I think I can depend upon
　　you.

Lamotte. You may, my Lord, securely—Is
　　there aught
Yet lies within my power to further what
Your passion may intend on Adeline?

Marquis. Nothing. It was not for a theme
　　like that
I ask'd this conference.

Lamotte. What then, my Lord?

Marquis. Tell me, my friend, for it excites
　　surprize,
How one like you, with powers by no means
　　humble,
Has thus been driv'n from Paris and your friends?

Lamotte. My Lord, with plainness and with
　　truth I'll tell you.
My means for ever sunk below my wishes—
I languish'd still for splendour out of reach,
Never by industry to be obtain'd.
I added fraud, at length, in all the forms
By which the sharper preys on inexperience.
Confederate with a bold and lawless band,
In time detection found us—Justice soon
Grown weary of protecting barefac'd guilt,
Pursued us to our ruin—I escap'd

Her fangs, and hop'd by time to soothe her fury.

Marquis. Could there no way be found to make your peace
At home? If it be in the scope of friendship,
You may command my fortune and my int'rest
In your atonement to the parties injur'd.

Lamotte. Your generosity, my Lord, o'erpow'rs me.
Would but the means could offer to my wish,
That I might shew my gratitude in deeds,
And spare these idle words.

Marquis. My worthy friend,
Such means do offer—They demand, indeed,
A mind superior to all common forms;
One prompt at friendship's bidding, to advance
The lingering step of vengeance.

Lamotte. Good, my Lord,
Speak plainly, and at once, what 'tis you point at;
It will not start me.

Marquis. Know, I have a foe;
Deadly, irreconcileably my foe.

Lamotte. O give him to my sword—this ready arm
Shall instant dare him to the field of death,
And rid my benefactor of his dread.

Marquis. Not so, Lamotte—This open-soul'd revenge
Has danger frequently to him who aims it.
The idle chivalry of modern manners

Allows the adversary, who has once
Committed injury, to add a second,
And slay the fool complaining for atonement.
The savage unperverted follows nature,
And stabs his unsuspecting enemy,
Pursues occasion of secure revenge,
And strikes the blow, when harmless to himself.

Lamotte. Say on, my Lord..

Marquis. No one, I think, observes us.

Lamotte. Not ev'n the zephyr stirs the trembling
   leaf,
All nature seems to pause.

Marquis. Nature! why, aye,
She pauses when her children's streaming blood
Moistens in death her most inhuman breast;
But ne'er takes cognizance of why they suffer.

Lamotte. I know her system is continued
   slaughter—
The strong devour the weak, and life is held
But by the tenure of surrounding groans.
Doubt not my zeal, nor aim thus to sustain
My rugged temper by such trite remark.
Whate'er your interest calls for on your foe,
By every power, or good, or bad, I'll do it.

Marquis. Then take this dagger.

Lamotte. How shall I employ it?

Marquis. Plunge it—

Lamotte. Where?

Marquis. Deep in the heart of Adeline.
                            [*Lamotte starts.*
Traitor, is this thy friendship?

Lamotte. Allow me but some moments of re-
    flection.
The death of Adeline! of her so lov'd,
Her whom you follow'd with such warmth of
    fondness?
Marquis. Aye. She is now the rancour of my
    peace,
And while she lives, plants daggers in my breast.
She must be dead, and instantly—Now answer.
Lamotte. My Lord, altho' the act with sudden
    horror
Startled my fix'd resolve, to do your bidding—
Yet shew me how it may be done with safety,
And I consent.
Marquis. Nothing more easy—thus.
My good Lamotte, it must be done this night.—
You can with ease enter her chamber, and
There rid me of my sole remaining fear—
I will return to-morrow, and then think
How I can best reward my kindest friend.
Lamotte. Conclude it done, my Lord.
Marquis. Lamotte, good day.   [*Exit.*
Lamotte. O most accomplish'd villain! wretched
    slave!
There can be no alternative but this—
Or she must be destroy'd—or I shall perish.
Behold the miserable lot of guilt!
One crime but pulls another on our heads,
And still the last is weightier than the former.
O, never let the luxury of life

Seduce weak man from the fix'd rules of honour!
From meanness, guilt is never far remov'd;
The tide of hell-born passions swells within him,
And whelms the soul in fathomless perdition.
                                    [*Exit.*

THE END OF THE FOURTH ACT.

ACT V.

SCENE—*The Forest.* (*Moonlight.*)

Enter MARQUIS.

Marquis.

WHEN can ambition lay him down secure
Of ill-got power, and dread no retribution?
While one slave lives who minister'd his purpose,
He is not safe—Witness that curs'd Laval—
The villain started not to slay his prince
At my command—but for the infant child,
He spar'd her to defeat my proudest hopes.
She lives in Adeline—Furies of Hell!
To tempt me thus with damning incest too!
And bid me crush the form I would enjoy!
Jaques! How now? What! Have you found
    Laval?

Enter JAQUES.

Jaques. No, my good Lord, nor heard late ti-
    dings of him.—
His townsmen say he left the country suddenly;
And since he went, nothing has e'er occur'd
To lead them to the knowledge of his course.
  Marquis. Make more enquiries still—He must
    be found,
And silenc'd by the only certain means.

I

Lamotte may play me false—If so, he dies;
And this firm hand shall seal down Adeline
In sleep eternal—Jaques, command your fellows
To guard the lanes that issue from the wood—
And on their lives, permit no one to pass.
If they do intercept, during the night,
Any thing human, see the fugitive
Be reconducted to the abbey yonder,
For there I shall expect you.

 Jaques. Well, my Lord.   [*Exeunt.*

 SCENE—*The Hall. A small Gate seen.*

 Enter LAMOTTE *and* MADAME.

 Madame. Why have you left your chamber thus,
  my husband;
Wherefore these haggard looks, as though despair
Usurp'd the seat of murderous suggestion?
Your vacant eye rolls its still cheated sense,
And you seem wrapt in horror.

 Lamotte. Frenzy, wife,
Presses upon my brain—Hark, some one knocks!
Look out! It is the Marquis! Lo! He comes!
In fierce resentment punishes my pity,
And now I cannot save her.

 Madame. No one comes;
Thro' the still abbey not a murmur breathes.

 Lamotte. My sense returns—make haste, my
  Adeline!
Oh save me, by thy flight, eternal pangs!
She comes! She comes!

Enter ADELINE *and* PETER.

Lamotte. Peter, is all prepared?
Give me the cloak—this will be neceſſary;
The weather elſe will chill my angel! There!
Peter, be ſure you take the road to Paris.

Peter. I know a narrow unfrequented track
That leads out to the road—the way's direct.

Madame. Adieu, dear Adeline!

Adeline. My beſt of parents!

Lamotte. Enquire Nemours out on arrival there—
Nay, no leave taking! we have not a moment.

[*Exeunt Adeline and Peter.*

Madame. Alas! Lamotte, I tremble to enquire
The cauſe of this confuſion—but our Adeline—

Lamotte. Was on the precipice's very verge,
And but this flight, no power here could ſave her.
Hortenſia, O thou never wilt believe
To what a wretch accurs'd, thy fate has join'd thee.
I pledg'd my hopes, my life to yonder Marquis,
To murder her this night.

Madame. Whom, Adeline?
Her you ſo lately ſnatch'd from brutal force?

Lamotte. Ev'n her. There's ſuch a coil around
    me, wife,
That, not to have done it, may be fatal to us—
Know, that to ſave thee from the gripe of hunger,
One fatal morn I ruſh'd into that wood
Bent upon plunder—Damning infamy
Soon pointed out a ſubject, and he prov'd—

Madame. The Marquis of Montault—Thou, good Lamotte,
Thus goaded by a villain, how I grieve
That confidence denied me, should thus sink thee!
Oh, never let one wedded wanderer blush
To give his errors to connubial trust!
The bosom of a wife's a sanctuary,
Where sad confession may repose his weakness,
And thence derive comfort that leads to virtue.

Lamotte. I own my error; dearest love, forgive me.

Madame. What's best now to be done?

Lamotte. Fly with the dawn.
I dare not meet the Marquis.

Madame. Yet, at worst,
His fear of your disclosure may preserve you.

Lamotte. Well thought on. Come, we'll make short preparation;
Then, if this savage, eager after blood,
Roam not the forest, 'ere the peep of day,
We'll trust ourselves on foot to mercy's care.

Madame. I shall not feel fatigue while you are happy.

As they are going out, enter the MARQUIS.

Marquis. Lamotte! Well, my friend;
　　　　　　　　　　　[*Exit Madame.*
Say, am I happy—hast thou done the deed?

Lamotte. I have, my Lord—Here Adeline wakes no more.
The fiercest spirit of the murdering fiends,
I think inspir'd me.

Marquis. Friendship such as this
Demands the warmest gratitude; command me,
And all my fortune's means to do you service.

Lamotte. But hear the manner of it—In her bed
She lay all discompos'd by Fancy's visions,
And in her sleep she call'd on me by name;
Implor'd my pity, and besought my aid .
To snatch her from the power of you, her tyrant.
I bade her wake, and thunder'd in her ear,
'Twas in your cause I came thus to destroy her.
Would you had seen her then! In rage I rush'd,
Enring'd these fingers in her golden hair,
And plung'd the thirsting poniard in her breast;
She struggled not—forgave me—and expir'd.

Marquis. Ha! this o'erstrain'd description bids
    me doubt him.   *(Aside.)*
Where is the body?—Bring me to the place.

Lamotte. My Lord, for fear of a discovery,
I cramm'd it into an old chest within
Which seem'd before to have serv'd the same oc-
    casion,
And buried it in haste, without your orders,
Deep in a cave, hard by here in the forest.

Marquis. What should I think! Jaques not yet
    return'd—
Yes, here he comes.   *(Goes to him.)*

Enter JAQUES.

Well, have you captur'd any?

Jaques. A lady and an old man seiz'd on horse-
    back.

Marquis. Conduct them to our presence in-
  stantly.   [*Exit Jaques.*
Impudent villain! thy high-labour'd tale
Gave thee at every word the clearest falsehood;
But I have other proof.—Thou hast dispatched her
With Peter through the forest.—
 Lamotte. Well, I own it.
I know the greatest peril of the act;
The die is thrown, and I abide the hazard.
 Marquis. Wretch, whom my foolish mercy
  once has spar'd,
Hope not to 'scape again thy just deserts.
Thy life is in my power, and by my vengeance
Shall expiate the robbery on our person.
 Lamotte. I fear you not.—Proclaim your ac-
  cusation,
Ev'n on the instant, I will brand your honour
With the seduction of my soul to murder.
 Marquis. Do so.—Thou wretched fool, who
  will believe thee?
When grac'd with all the eloquence of rank,
I stand to answer to the sullied charge
Made by an outlaw'd gambler, and a robber,
Can you e'er hope it will be credited?
 Lamotte. If I have sav'd her, I shall die with
  transport.
 Marquis. See her brought back to thank thee
  for that saying.

Enter ADELINE, *and* PETER *guarded.*

Adeline. O, good Lamotte, my wretched fate has funk thee!
How shall I bear to see my injur'd mother!

Enter MADAME.

Madame. What horror meets me.—Adeline return'd!

Marquis. Madam, retire—the strict demands of justice
Have too much terror, when they reach a husband. [*Madame about to supplicate.*

Lamotte. Hortensia, not one word in my behalf!
I go to answer to offended justice;
But, Marquis, should thy fatal thirst of blood
Persist in the design to me entrusted,
Unheard of miseries must await such outrage.

Marquis. Bear her to close confinement instantly.

Madame. Never, my lovely child, my darling friend,
O, I can never lose thee! Man of terrors,
I charge thee, see thou wound not innocence
Pure as the shrines of saints.

Marquis. Bear off the women!
In separate chambers see them strictly guarded.
[*Taken apart.*
Seize you that ruffian—Lo, the very wretch,
Who lately robb'd us in the wood adjacent.

Enter LOUIS.

Louis. Hold off your hands, you servile Ministers,
Or my quick rage shall trample you to earth.
　Marquis. Audacious stripling! know, within my power
Is placed the fate of yonder wretched plunderer.
Or give my pleasure way, or thou thyself,
Rash Minion, shalt repent this bold intrusion.
　Louis. What, is it thus in France? that a foul murderer,
Harden'd in crimes himself, and stain'd with blood,
Shall deal his sentence out on virtuous men,
And write his ruffian vengeance in their hearts!
O soil accurs'd! I know thee then no more.
　Marquis. Insolent villain! Silence for thy life!
　Louis. My life is plac'd under too high a guard
For the assassin's steel to reach at it.
It is devoted to disclose thy crimes,
And so appease a murder'd brother's shade.
Come forth, Nemours!

Enter NEMOURS.

　Marquis. Now, Sir, what make you here?
　Nemours. Behold in me the delegate express
E'en from thy Sovereign—vested with the powers
To bring thee straight to answer to a charge

Of most unnatural murder.—If thou refuse,
A guard at hand shall drag thee to our courts.
      [*Enter a guard behind.*

 Marquis. Sir, as a minister of justice, sent
With powers I must respect, I yield in all things.
But may I ask what proofs you have of this,
Which boldly I pronounce a falsehood? Say,
Did not yon boy provoke this fond procedure?

 Nemours. So far you're right: He did, and on
  sure grounds.

 Marquis. You will not think so, when you hear
  my tale;
Know that his father robb'd our very person,
For which offence, no doubt, this wretched plot
Was hatch'd against my honour and my life;
But Justice shall avenge me on them all.

 Nemours. Sir, you deceive yourself—Lo, here
  a witness,
Even in your brother's hand, whereby he charges
You and your slaves suborn'd, with his arrest
Here in the very Abbey.

 Marquis. Forgery all.
By Heav'n, my brother fell in Hungary,
A valiant champion for the Holy Cross.

 Nemours. Nay, 'tis no late imposture—View it
  well!
Its characters obliterated half,
And faded what remain, by time and damps.

 Marquis. Sir, I affirm again 'tis desperate forgery.
      K

Give me a living witness to confront me.

Nemours. Know you one, nam'd Laval? What, does it shake thee?

Enter LAVAL.

See the wretch brought before thee.

Marquis. Furies seize him!

Lamotte. By Heav'n, the very man who gave me Adeline!

Marquis. Then I am caught indeed! O that my rage
Could crush, at once, mankind in general ruin.
No! tho' all hell seems arm'd against my life,
I will not yield me to your torturing ruffians,
Nor, like a slave, expire upon a scaffold.
This way alone, does not degrade ambition.
[*Stabs himself and falls.*

Lamotte. Desperate to the last.

Nemours. A dreadful judgment.
[*He makes a sign, and exit Laval.*

Marquis. The hand of death has clear'd my cheated sight—
Lamotte, draw nearer, and mark my latest words—
I have done all I'm charg'd with; Adeline
Is that wrong'd brother's child—I know it—
Most horrible conviction made it certain—
All that I have is hers.—Is so by right,
I would not now withhold it! Could she forgive me!
But that's impossible.—O mercy, Heaven!
[*Dies.*

Louis. My Adeline! [*Kneels.*
Madame. My husband thus restor'd,
My darling son the means too!
Nemours. Even so;
Lamotte, a secret Providence, no doubt,
Directed this disclosure—That Laval,
About to suffer for another crime,
Begg'd respite to disclose this scene of horrors.
Your son arrived to give it truth undoubted.
  Lamotte: Joy beams at length on all but me, sincere,
Pure and unclouded; but my penitence
Will, I trust, expiate my former errors,
And chear the exile they have forc'd upon me.
  Nemours. Lamotte, for you a brighter prospect dawns,
Nor shall your future days be dimm'd with sorrow.
The King, to recompense the valiant deeds
Of your brave son, recalls you to your home,
And with free pardon blots out past offences.
  Lamotte. My son! my son! I have no words to thank thee. [*Embraces him.*
  Nemours. For you, dear Lady, justice has prepar'd
The full possession of your lineal rights:
  Adeline. 'Tis here I owe their splendour; and thus pay
The gratitude at once for life and love.
                [*Gives her hand to Louis.*

Madame. My children, may superior joys await ye,
And lengthen out a date of mutual fondness.

Adeline. My worthy venerable guide, to you
I'm bound for such advent'rous sympathy
As scorn'd the claims of age, to save a stranger.

Peter. I see you innocent and happy, Madam;
The best reward that I can hope on earth.

Adeline. The great Avenger of perverted nature
Before us has display'd a solemn lesson,
How he dispels the cloud of mystery,
With which the sinful man surrounds his crimes;
It calls us to adore in awful wonder,
And reccommend ourselves by humble virtue.

[*Exeunt omnes.*

THE END.

EPILOGUE

TO FONTAINVILLE FOREST,

BY THE AUTHOR OF THE PLAY,

FOR MRS. POPE.

WELL, heav'n be prais'd, I have escap'd at last,
And all my woman's doubts and fears are past.
Before this awful crisis of our play,
Our vent'rous bard has often heard me say—
Think you, our friends, one modern ghost will see,
Unless, indeed, of Hamlet's pedigree:
Know you not, Shakspeare's petrifying pow'r
Commands alone the horror-giving hour?

" Madam, said he, with mingled awe and love;
" I think of Him, the brightest spirit above,
" Who triumphs over time and fickle forms;
" The changes of caprice, and passion's storms;
" Whose mighty muse the subject world must bind,
" While sense and nature charm the willing mind."

But Sir, I cry'd, your eulogy apart,
Which flows from mine, indeed from every heart.
You mean to sanction then your own pale sprite,
By his " that did usurp this time of night:"
" I do, he answer'd, and I beg you'll spare
" My injur'd phantom ev'ry *red*-sea pray'r:
" Why should your terror *lay* my proudest boast,
" Madam I die, if I give up the ghost."

EPILOGUE.

The jest which bursted from his motley mind,
Anxious as it must be, has made me kind;
I come his advocate, if there be need,
And give him *absolution* for the deed.
You'll not deny my spiritual power,
But let me rule at least one little hour!
Be your's the sceptre every future day,
And mine the transport humbly to obey.

www.ingramcontent.com/pod-product-compliance
Lightning Source LLC
Chambersburg PA
CBHW022144090426
42742CB00010B/1390